Say It

&

Have It

Decrees, Affirmations, Confessions and Declarations of
Faith for Locating Hope, Sustaining it and Turning it to
the Reality of Strong Faith that Births Victories, Liberty,
Breakthroughs and Testimonies.

Munachimso Nwosu

Say It & Have It

Copyright © 2016 Munachimso Nwosu

Tel: +234-8028383477

Email: network4helpers@gmail.com

Unless otherwise indicated, all scripture quotations are from the authorized King James Version of the Holy Bible (KJV).

First Published by Global Reach Publishing LLC 2016

ISBN: 9785049612
ISBN-13: 978-9785049619

Printed in the United States of America

To God Be the Glory, Great Things He has done.

DEDICATION

To my family,

My wife Chijindu Patience.

My Children Zoe, David (*Munachi Jr*) and Oganihu

May you all achieve divine purpose and maximize God's providence in life.

"*Our words are powerful tools... Our words are powerful commands to the fabrics and mechanisms of heaven, the earth and the universe to spring into action, and deliver on demand our inheritance for the materialization of divine destiny.*"

- Munachimso Nwosu

CONTENTS

ACKNOWLEDGMENTS

I appreciate my wife Chijindu who understood my long hours of work that often affected my attention to her and was supportive.

My gratitude goes to my friend Kalu Igwe Kalu who inspired and motivated me to complete this work and further mentors me for greater success and fulfillment.

The sources that produced the reference points for this work Dr. Creflo Dollar, Rev. Kenneth Hagin of blessed memory, Charles Capps, who have all been my life long teachers and mentors as I apply their teachings in all areas of my life, I am grateful.

My appreciation to all other God sent helpers in my growth, journey in life such as Bro Kenneth Copeland and Bishop (*Papa*) David Oyedepo who taught me overcoming faith. Pastor Tony Rapu who taught me prayer and Christian innovation, Pastor Enoch (*Daddy GO*) Adeboye, Rev. Tony Akinyemi for integrity and holiness, and other mentors inclusive of

Elder Ernest Mbanefo.

I appreciate and pray for God's blessing on all men and women in Christian ministry, Christian congregations and pastors worldwide too numerous to mention, Evangelist Reinhardt Bonnke, Evangelist Uma Ukpai, Pastor Annie Ikebudu, Rev Anyanwu (*AGA*). The members and trustees of my NGO/ministry.

My parents and siblings. I appreciate Chinyere Nledum who diligently typed and arranged this work. Lastly, I praise, thank and worship my eternal father God, My Redeemer and intercessor Jesus Christ, the Holy Spirit who are the originators and commissioners of this work and my mission on Earth. My angels and spiritual supports of heaven, I am open to your ministrations on my life path and journey.

Munachimso Nwosu

CHAPTER ONE

INTRODUCTION

O ur words are powerful tools for carrying out our destiny as delivered by God. God himself started creation with words which sprang to life.

Genesis 1:2, 3

Despite the challenges of a desolate, formless void, his spoken words bought newness, order, form, beauty and harmony. He as our father expects nothing less from us as creatures who have received a measure of faith. Faith is amplified by words. Visions and plans are materialized by words.

Our words are powerful commands to the fabrics and mechanisms of heaven, the earth and the universe to spring into action to deliver on demand our inheritance for the materialization of divine destiny.

In the spiritual, mental and physical forms of life to see, believe and then give utterance to it actually sends a command to facilitating forces and entities such as angels, the Holy Spirit, man and associated creation to combine forces to assist us.

By the meticulous application of the spoken word, decrees are enforced for breakthroughs, miracles, breaking of barriers, removal of curses, healing, manifestation of victory, successes etc. We also reprogram our conscious and subconscious mind. This book guides you to program and set in motion every aspect of your life and your circumstances for a turn around.

Among faith filled and practicing Christian believers, the efficacy of the spoken word is proven. It's creative and powerful. Become excited in this path and see challenges under your feet.

HOW TO USE THIS BOOK

In this book you will find in the chapters definite headings peculiar to your situation, meditate on the words and settle in your heart the authority available to you as given by the restoration of your rightful place in God, read out the particular words for the particular situation and in the course of time, if done daily (*morning and evening*) and consistently despite the size of the expectation, increasing crisis or enormity of the problem you will experience relief and transformation over time(*Read out loud preferably placing your name within e.g. I ---------- receive health, You can also listen to the audio version while on the go in the car, through other media devices and at Night.*) This is the right way, which even the negative forces and their agencies try to mimic to their seeming advantage. In application, access to this benefits starts by relocating from the kingdom of curses to that of blessing. From sin to righteousness (*see prayer below*).Prior to the declarations, start off with Prayer of thanks giving, praises and worship, Pray in tongues (*where possible for some time*) then call your angels and the holy spirit to take your words and materialize them. Read out morning and late evening (you can also write out your declarations and projects and carry them in pocket pieces or hang/paste on the wall where you will see it) as the severity of the challenge arises or the expectation. Read out in whole or in part as you can. Afterward thank God and believe that before expected date your desire will come, (I usually set a three months window). Keep praising God, never murmur, complain or speak negatively.

You can also agree with a partner on the said project. Have the mindset of a sower who will eventually get his/her harvest. Also be sensitive to the leading of the Holy Spirit as regards necessary actions, sacrifices and strategies to carry out. Don't procrastinate promptings Also be sensitive to your dream life, vision, inward witness, the word, revelations, etc. as God will guide you towards your breakthrough and miracle.

However, this is not to excuse the relevance of hard work, diligence or orderly health habits and life, vision, a life anchored on God, believing, obeying and living in tandem with his will is the sure guarantee for success, a right to victory, so start with the most important confession of all (if you are not yet a believer in Jesus Christ). Say this out loud and in sincerity.

"Lord Jesus I am a sinner. I believe

you died on the cross of Calvary over two thousands years ago, to save me from my sins... I believe you shed your blood that I may live. I accept you as my Lord and Master. Therefore from today I am saved, I am born again, old things are gone. I am now new."

Congratulations if you have prayed this prayer and welcome to a new world of possibilities.

- Munachimso Nwosu

CHAPTER TWO

MIND RENEWAL, WISDOM, PEACE & SPIRITUAL DEVELOPMENT

1.   I am in Christ, therefore I am a new creature, and the life of the past is no longer an influence over me.

2.   I have eternal life; the very nature of God is in me, developing me to greater glory.

3.   I tap into the life of God and progress beyond natural ability to supernatural ability.

4.   The supernatural life of God has come into me, the life of God is on the inside of me, and it is the light and wisdom for my life.

5.   Eternal life is working in me right now, eternal life is working in me and destroying bondages and breaking yokes.

6.   I am the light of the world, a city that is set upon the hill that cannot be hidden. Matt 5:13

7.   The life of God resides on the inside of me. Eternal life is working in me right now.

8.   The Zoë life of God is affecting my mind and making me smarter. Zoë life of God is now granting me wisdom.

9.   The life of God is enlightening me. The life of God is granting me wisdom.

10. I am a co-creator with God, calling those things that be not as if they were.

11. Eternal life is working in me now and always, therefore I am operating on a higher level. I exist on a higher level.

12. I have access to a higher life, the eternal life.

13. This world cannot limit me; I am a citizen of heaven.

14. The nature of God is developing me above the life of the flesh, I am supernatural. I am not subject to the things in the natural, they are subject to me.

15. Eternal life is working in me, eternal life; God's own nature is working on me and on the outside of me.

16. God's life and light is dominating every part of me.

17. Eternal life of God is taking me to a higher life.

18. I receive spiritual insight. Above all circumstances of life.

19. I receive the Holy natures of God.

20. I have the spirit of wisdom. I have the spirit of understanding.

21. I have the spirit of might. I have the spirit of power.

22. The feeling of love is the highest frequency, I emit it.

23. I am the master of my thoughts.

24. I will lay hands on the sick and they will recover, therefore I possess healings for the oppressed.

25. I have God's power to reign in life.

26. O Lord, make me know the ways of life and make me full of joy.

27. I am seated far above, all principalities and powers together with Christ above-all satanic powers.

28. I have authority through Christ over the earth.

29. I am established in Christ and anointed by God.

30. I live in Gods power; I live in the spirit of faith. I have the spirit of faith.

31. I am redeemed from the kingdom of darkness, I exercise my heavenly authority.

32. I have eternal life of God according to *1 John 2:25.*

33. The Lord will keep me from falling and will present me faultless before His presence – *Jude 24.*

34. I have the spirit of faith. I believe the word; therefore as I speak it, I am a member of the household of faith. God has given to me a measure of faith. I never speak of doubt, for I am a believer the word is near me, in my heart and in my mouth through the word of faith, I am a victor, because faith is the victory.

35. I am the righteousness of God in Christ Jesus.

36. Giving thanks to the father who has qualified us (me) to be partakers of the

inheritance of the saints in the light. He has delivered us (me) from the power of darkness and conveyed me (us) into the kingdom of the son of His love in whom we have redemption through His blood, the forgiveness of sins – *Col. 1:12-14.*

37. I am an heir of God and a joint heir with Jesus Christ. I am not a captive of Satan.

38. I am blessed with every spiritual blessing, the father himself loves me. *Eph. 1:3.*

39. In God (Him) I live, move and have my being. *Acts. 17:28.*

40. I have the same spirit that worked in the prophets of old, I have the spirit of Elijah (might) spirit of wisdom in Daniel; I have the spirit of favor and influence that worked in Joseph.

41. I can do all things through Christ who empowers me from within. *Phil. 4:13.*

42. I am chosen by the act of redemption to be Jesus Christ messenger.

43. God has chosen me to be His own, through what Christ would do for me he decided to make me Holy in His eyes without a single fault; I stand before Him covered with His love. *Eph. 1:4.*

44. I am adopted into God's family through Christ.

45. My heart is full of light from the Lord and my behavior and character show it. *Eph. 5:8.*

46. I learn what pleases God and I take no part in the worthless pleasures of evil and darkness, but instead I rebuke and expose them. *Eph. 5:10.*

47.   I am filled with the Holy Spirit and I am controlled by Him.

48.   My strength comes from the mighty power of God within me. *Eph. 6:10.*

49.   I am chosen by God to be his representative on earth, to bring deliverance to many. *Rom. 1:4.*

50.   I have the Holy natures of God himself at work in me. *Rom. 1:4.*

51.   I have been made right in God's sight by faith in His promises. I have real peace with God because of what Jesus has done for me.

52.   God loves me and I feel his warm love everywhere within me, because he has given me His spirit to fill my heart with His love. *Rom. 5:5.*

53. I have right standing with God and eternal life through Jesus Christ my Lord. *Rom. 5:21.*

54. There is no condemnation for those who belong to Christ Jesus for the power of the life giving Spirit through Jesus have freed me from the vicious circle of sin & death. *Rom. 8:1-2.*

55. I actively obey God's laws by following after the Holy Spirit. I no longer follow the flesh.

56. I follow after God; I am no longer controlled by my lower natures. *Rom. 8: 5 - 6.*

57. I am controlled by the spirit of God living inside me. *Rom. 8:9.*

58. I am a son of God because I am led by the spirit. *Rom. 8:15.*

59.   I have God's wisdom & strength within me.

60.   Heavenly father, I thank you that I am a believer; I am a child of God. I have been born again. I am born of God. Thou art my own father. I am thy very own child. It is written beloved thou art a child of God. I am a child of God. Thank you. My father, because it is also written in thy Holy word "greater is He that is in you. The greater one is in me. It is also written I am the temple of the living God. As God has said I will dwell, I will live in them. I will walk in them. They will be my people, I will be their God. Oh Lord, creator of heaven & earth, thou art my God, thou dost live in me. Greater is he that is in me, than he that is in the world.

61. I am a child of the infinite life which knows no end, and I am a child of eternity of God. I am wonderful.

62. I am of God and have overcome Him (Satan) for greater is he that is in me than he that is in the world. *1 John 4:4.*

63. I am an overcomer and I overcome by the blood of the lamb and the word of my testimony. *Rev. 12:11.*

64. I am submitted to God and the devil flees from me because I resist Him in the name of Jesus. *James. 4:7.*

65. The word of God is forever settled in heaven; therefore I establish His word upon this earth. *Psalm 119:89.*

66. And I, having received the gift of righteousness do reign as a king in life by Jesus Christ. *Rom. 5:17.*

67. The Spirit of truth abideth in me and teaches me all things, and guides me into all truths. Therefore, I confess I have perfect knowledge of every situation and circumstance. I come up against, for I have the wisdom of God. *John 16:13; James 1:5.*

68. In all my ways I acknowledge Him and he directs my path. *Pro. 3:6.*

69. The Lord will perfect that which concerneth me – *Psalm 138:8.*

70. I let the word of Christ dwell in me richly in all wisdom. *Col. 3:16.*

71. I do follow the good shepherd and I know His voice, and the voice of a stranger I will not follow. *John 10:4 – 5*

72. Jesus is made unto me wisdom, righteousness, sanctification, and redemption, therefore I confess I have the wisdom of God, and I am the righteousness

of God in Christ Jesus. *(1Cor. 1:30; 2Cor. 5:21).*

73.	I am filled with the knowledge of the Lord's will in all wisdom and spiritual understanding. *Col. 1:9.*

74.	I am a new creation in Christ, I am His workmanship, created in Christ Jesus, therefore, I have the mind of Christ and the wisdom of God is formed within me. *2 Cor.5:17; Eph. 2:10; 1 Cor. 2:16.*

75.	I am set apart for God. I am accepted by God through what Christ has done for me. *1Cor. 6:11.*

76.	I Receive the Holy Spirit as a partner; I receive His gifts for services to God. Holy Spirit you are welcome to my life, take charge of me.

77. Holy Spirit display your power, God's power through me as a man for helping the entire church and fulfilling ministry.

78. The love of God is poured out in my heart by the Holy Spirit (therefore I possess the ability to love everyone).

79. The Lord will never leave nor forsake me (therefore I possess the presence of God with each step I take at all times. *Heb. 13:5.*

80. I am the redeemed of the Lord (therefore I possess redemption benefits everyday. *Ps. 107:2; Rev. 5:9.*

81. I am the righteous who is as bold as a lion (therefore I possess lion hearted boldness in spiritual warfare. *Pro. 28:1*

82. I am a branch of the living vine (Christ) therefore; I possess vine life wherever I go. *John 15:5.*

83. I have God's power to reign in life.

84.　I am the righteousness of God in Him *(2 Cor. 5:21).* Therefore, I possess the ability to stand freely in God's holy presence and in Satan's presence a victor.

85.　I am the temple of the living God *(2 Cor. 6:16)* therefore I possess the reality of God dwelling in me and walking in me.

86.　God has made me Holy in His eyes, without a single fault, I stand before Him covered with His love. *Eph. 1:4.*

87.　I have been adopted into the family of God through the death of Christ for me. *Eph. 1:5.*

88.　I command ministering angels to operate in all area of my life and bring me fully to God's plans and purposes for my life.

89.　I yield my life to be a witness of the resurrection of Christ.

90. I am led by the Holy Spirit, not the Law of Moses.

91. I think, speak, and act lovingly, quietly and peacefully.

92. God is life and this life is flowing through me at this moment and always.

93. God is expressing himself, as harmony, peace, beauty, joy and abundance through me.

94. I am wise in the way of divine life; I am happy radiant, successful, serene and powerful.

95. I am a child of the infinite life which knows no end, and I am a child of heaven's eternity. I am created wonderful.

96. I am complete in Him who is the head of all principalities and power for I am His workmanship created in Christ Jesus unto good works which God has before

ordained that I should walk therein. *Col. 2:10.*

97. I let no corrupt communication proceed out of my mouth, but that which is good to edifying, that it may minister grace to the hearer, I grieve not the Holy Spirit of God, whereby I'm sealed unto the day of redemption. *Eph. 4:29.*

I receive the best of the land of Goshen and I will eat the fat of the land. (Name the city)

98. I speak the truth of the word of God in love and I grow up into the Lord Jesus Christ in all things. *Eph. 4:15.*

99. I am born of God and I have world overcoming faith residing on the inside of me, for greater is He that is in me than He that is in the world. *(1 John 5:4, 4; 1 John 4:4).*

100. I have put off the old man and put on the new man, who is renewed in the knowledge after the image of Him that created me – *Col. 3:10.*

101. I receive the Spirit of wisdom and revelation in the knowledge of Him, the eyes of my understanding being enlightened. And I am not conformed to this world but am transformed by the renewing of my mind. My mind is renewed by the word of God *(Eph. 1:17, 18; Rom. 12:2).*

102. I am increasing in the knowledge of God daily, moment by moment. I am strengthened with all might according to His glorious power. *Col. 1:10, 11.*

103. And I having received the gift of righteousness do reign as a king in life by Christ Jesus. *Rom. 5:17.*

104. The word of God is forever settled in heaven; therefore, I establish His word upon this earth *(Ps. 119:89).*

105. Jesus became he curse; so that I may be blessed therefore I am blessed to be a blessing in life.

106. I have the covenant (promise) of His blood to cleanse me from all sins through the sacrifice of Christ.

107. I am of a chosen generation, a royal priesthood, a Holy nation, God's own special people, that I may proclaim the praises of Him who called me out of darkness into His marvelous light *(1Peter. 2:9).*

108. I have been made a king and priest to my God. *(Rev. 5:10).*

109. I am an imitator of God, I talk like Him and act like Him.

110. I am capable of doing all that God asks me to do.

111. I believe and trust that Jesus gave Himself for our sins that He might deliver us from this present evil world according to the will of God and our father, I am therefore made righteous to live in Holiness, I live in Holiness (bear the fruit of holiness).

112. I walk in full agreement with the pattern of good works which God has ordained I should work in. I am built up to be a habitation of God through His Spirit.

113. I hold on fast to the profession of my faith without wavering, for He is faithful that promised. *Heb. 10:23.*

114. Whatsoever things are true, whatsoever things are honest, whatsoever things are just, whatsoever things are pure, whatsoever things are lovely, whatsoever things are of good report, if there be any virtue, and if there be any praise, I think on these things. *Philippians 4:8.*

115. And you (me) that were sometime alienated and enemies in your (my) mind by wicked works yet now hath he reconciled. In the body of His flesh through death to present you (me) Holy and unblameable and unreproveable in his sight. *Col. 1:21-22.*

116. I lay apart all filthiness and superfluity of naughtiness and receive with meekness the engrafted word which is able to save my

soul. I am a doer of the word and not hearers only, deceiving my own self.

117.   Whereby are given unto us (*me*) exceeding great and precious promises, that by those ye might be partakers of the divine nature, having escaped the corruption that is in the world through lust.

118.   I shall also decree a thing and it shall be established unto me.

119.   I am a doer of the word of God and am blessed in my deeds. I am happy in those things I do because I am a doer of the word of God. *James 1:22.*

120.   I am ever grateful, so grateful for what God has done, is doing and is going to do for me.

CHAPTER THREE

PEACE

1. The peace of God reigns in my spirit, mind and body.

2. The peace of God guarantees me health, prosperity and progress.

3. The peace of God in my life surmounts fear, doubt, worry and all the weapons of the enemy.

4. I give thanks to Christ for my good health.

5. I give thanks to God for my prosperous and wealthy life.

6. I give thanks for being alive and not dead.

7. Christ has redeemed me from the spiritual death I have eternal life.

8. I let the word of God dwell in me richly in all wisdom. *Col. 3:16.*

9. Wisdom has entered my heart and knowledge is pleasant to my soul, discretion

will preserve me and understanding will keep me to deliver me from the way of evil.

10. I shall decree a thing and it shall be established unto me and the light shall shines upon my ways. *Job. 22:28.*

11. I lay apart all filthiness and superfluity of naughtiness and l receive with meekness the engrafted word which is able to save my soul.

12. Let the word of Christ dwell in me richly in all wisdom; teaching and admonishing one another in psalms and hymns and spiritual songs, singing with grace in my heart to the Lord. *Col. 3:16.*

13. That I might walk worthy of the Lord unto all pleasing, being fruitful in every good work, and increasing in this knowledge of God. *Col. 1:10.*

14. I am the salt of the earth, I shall not lose my flavor- Matt 5:13

CHAPTER FOUR

SPIRITUAL & MENTAL DELIVERANCE, VICTORY, DIVINE PROTECTION, FREEDOM FROM FEAR/WORRY, ETC.

1. I am the body of Christ and Satan has no power over me. For I overcome evil with good – *1 Cor. 12:27, Rom. 12:21.*

2. I will fear no evil for thou art with me lord, your word and your spirit they comfort me – *Ps. 23:4*

3. I am far from any spiritual, mental oppression, fear does not come near me – *Isa. 54:14*

4. I am delivered from the evils of this present world for it is the will of God for me – *Gal. 1:14*

5. No evil will befall me neither shall any plague come nigh my dwelling. For the Lord has given His angels charge over me

and they keep me in all my ways and in my pathway is life, there is no death (also for safety while traveling) – *Ps. 91:10, 11; Prov.12:28*

6. I take the shield of faith and quench every fiery dart that the wicked one brings against me – *Eph. 6:16.*

7. I am an overcomer and I overcome by the Blood of the Lamb and the word of my testimony – *Rev. 12:11*

8. I am submitted to God and the devil flees from me because I resist him in the name of Jesus – *James 4:7*

9. Christ has redeemed me from the curse of the law, Christ has redeemed me from spiritual death and all the wiles of the enemy

10. I do follow the good shepherd; I know His voice and the voice of a stranger I will not follow – *John 10:4, 5.*

11. I am a new creation in Christ; I am His workmanship created in Christ Jesus. Therefore, I have the mind of Christ and the wisdom of God is formed within me – *2 Cor. 5:17; Eph. 2:10; 1 Cor. 2:16*

12. I receive the spirit of wisdom and revelation in the knowledge of Him. The eyes of my understanding being enlightened. And I am not conformed to this world but am transformed by the renewing of my mind. My mind is renewed by the Word of God – *Eph. 1:17, 18;   Rom. 12:2.*

13. I am increasing in the knowledge of God. I am strengthened with all might according to His glorious power – *Col. 1:10, 11*

14. I am delivered from the power of darkness and I am translated into the kingdom of His dear son - *Col. 1:13*

15. The joy of the Lord is my strength. The Lord is the strength of my life – *Neh. 8:10; Ps. 27:1.*

16. The peace of God which passeth all understanding keeps my heart and my mind through Christ Jesus, and things which are good, and pure, and perfect, and lovely, and of good report. I think on these things. *Phil. 4:7, 8*

17. No man shall take me out of His hand for I have eternal life – *John 10:29*

18. I let the peace of God rule on my heart and I refuse to worry about any thing – *Col. 3:15*

19. I am delivered from any satanic pit and snares, all arrows shot at me returns to sender. My head will not be sacrificed on

any evil altar; neither will it go for another. I shall not carry any yoke of evil upon my shoulders. The eyes of evil and envy are blinded for my sake. Any evil meeting against me is shattered by fire.

20. Whatever speaks lying vanities against me is shut up forever. No enchantment or contraption against me will prevail. I command my glorious destiny ordained by God before the foundation of the earth to manifest fully. All that is generational evil of any form ceases in my time. I cover my self and my seed in the Blood of Jesus, I am free. Whatever I know not or do in ignorance will no longer affect me. I am now a child of Zion.

21. God is on my side, God is in me now, who can be against me, He has given unto me all things that pertain unto life and Godliness.

Therefore am a partaker of His divine nature - *Rom. 8:31; 2nd Cor. 6:16, John 10:10.*

22. I am a believer and these signs of follow me in the name of Jesus. I overcome and cast out satan, demons and all nature of principalities and situations – *Mark. 16:17, 18.*

23. Jesus gave me the authority to use His name. And that which I bind on earth is bound in heaven. And that which I loose on earth is loosed in heaven. And therefore in the name of the Lord Jesus Christ I bind the principalities, the power, the rulers of darkness of this wicked world. I bind and cast down spiritual wickedness in high places and render them harmless and ineffective against me (or family) in the name of Jesus (For family deliverance etc) – *Matt. 16:19; John 16:23, 24; Eph. 6:12.*

24.   I ………….am complete in Him who is the head of all principality and power. For I am His workmanship created in Christ Jesus unto good work, which God has before ordained that I should walk therein – *Col. 2:10; Eph. 2:10*

25.   Christ has set me free, I am bonded to Christ, I am set free from sin, diseases and all the yokes of satan, for I am bought with a great price – *1ˢᵗ Cor. 7:22-23.*

26.   Jesus is Lord over my life. Jesus is Lord over my health so I will not be sick. Jesus is Lord over my business/career so I will prosper. Jesus is Lord over my marriage so it will not experience divorce but grow stronger and better. Jesus is Lord over………

27.   Jesus is my Lord, therefore I possess total salvation from any satanic force – *Rom.10:9-10.*

28. In the name of Jesus I cast out demons, therefore I possess dynamic deliverance over satans power – *Mark 16:17*

29. I am free from all forms of fear, worry etc. for God has not give us (me) a spirit of fear, but of power and of love and of a sound mind – *2 Tim.1:7*

30. Lord Jesus I thank you that I receive rest in all areas of my life such as in my health, finances, etc.

31. For my possession I shall break them with a rod of iron, I shall dash them (enemies) to pieces like a potters vessel.

32. I am delivered from all forms of barrenness drought and limitation. I am fruitful. I increase abundantly, multiplying and growing exceedingly mighty – *Exo. 1:7*

33. Father God I receive your power for victory by the entrance of the Holy Spirit in my life.

let all that is dead in my life be made alive now – Acts 1:8

34.   I command ministering angels to operate in all areas of my life, and bring me fully to Gods plan and purposes for my life.

35.   I have put on the whole armor of God that resist the enemy (satan). I am immune to all satanic and demonic strategies, tricks and forms of wickedness – *Eph. 6:11*

36.   I have total and continuous victory against all evil rulers of the unseen world and satanic and evil princes of darkness that rule this world, including wicked spirits.

CHAPTER FIVE

DELIVERANCE PRAYER

1. Lord Jesus Christ I believe that you are the son of God and the only way to God and on the cross you died for my sins and that you rose from the dead, that on the cross also you were made a curse that I might be redeemed from the curse and receive your blessing. I trust you now for mercy and forgiveness and I commit myself from now on to live by your grace to follow you and obey you, I ask you to forgive and blot out my sins committed by me or my ancestors that exposed me to this curse. If people has wronged me or harmed me, I forgive them as I would have God forgive me. I renounce all contacts with satan or with occults practices or with unscriptural secret societies, if I have any contact objects that link me to all in these kings, I promise to

destroy them, now with the authority given me as a child of God, I release myself from every curse that has ever come upon me or affected me in anyway in the name of Jesus – Amen.

2. Greater is He that lives within me, I am fortified from within, I am strengthened from within.

3. I am delivered from every spiritual, mental and physical shackles/yokes. I receive my health and I thank God for the restored health, finances, spirituality, children, career, etc.

4. In Jesus name, I declare and know that I have divine authority over the devil, therefore I exercise it.

5. I am an overcomer and destined by divine heritage to live a triumphant life.

6. The flood of evil has no power over me.

7. Any mark of the wicked one is removed from me today. I am immune to all satanic plans.

8. The force of poverty, disease and death is defeated in my life. I enter the purpose and inheritance of God for my life. I am freed from all spiritual, physical and mental shackles.

9. I/we am rescued by the hand and might of God. I am liberated unto the Glory of God above any spiritual barriers.

10. I neutralize any spell, divination, and enchantment by any witchcraft, curses of any evil man/woman and group on my life in Jesus name.

11. I refuse and bind any spirit of deception by satan over my life. I silence all lying vanities and spirit of the world in Jesus name.

12. In withstand in Jesus name all the wiles/deceptions of the devil and His agents over my life.

13. I receive the working knowledge of the truth of Christ in God that sets my mind and spirit free from every shackle.

14. I am the beloved of God, I cease to be molested by any evil force whatsoever on earth. I am a bride of Christ. God is jealous over me. I am precious in His sight.

15. Every evil arrow shot at me/us is back to sender. Every pit of evil dug to consume me removed, I step over it. I am released from every snare of destiny. The yoke is lifted from my shoulders. I shall not be a victim but a victor.

16. I am positioned in God righteousness, righteousness is a defense. I put on the breast plate of righteousness and all the whole

armor of God to withstand all fiery darts and attacks.

17. I have the spirit of faith I believe the word. Therefore as I speak it, I am a member of the household of faith. God has given me a measure of faith. I never speak of doubt, for I am a believer. The word is near me in my heart and in my mouth, through the word of faith; I am a victor because faith is the victory.

18. I am redeemed from the kingdom of darkness through the precious Blood of Jesus.

19. The Lord is always with me, even until the very end of life's journey – *Matt. 28:20*

PRAYER FOR DIVINE HELP/WARFARE

20. Lord there is no one like you to help the powerless against the mighty. Help us/me O Lord, for we/I rely on you and in your

name we have come against this vast army. Lord there is no one like you to help the powerless against the mighty, help us/me O Lord our God for we/I rely on you and in your name we have come against this vast army. O Lord you are our God, do not let man prevail against you – *2nd Chronicle 14:11*

21.   Lord you are a shield for me, my Glory and the lifter of my head.

CHAPTER SIX

SELF-DEFENCE SCRIPTURES

1. Lord God, I thank you for delivering me now and always from my strong enemy and from those who hated me – *Ps. 18:17*

2. No weapon formed against me/us shall prosper, and every tongue which rises against me/us in judgment shall condemn. This is the heritage of the servants of the Lord – *Isa. 54:17*

3. Blessed be the name of the Lord God for ever and ever, for wisdom and might are His, He changes the times and seasons, He removes kings and raises kings. He gave wisdom to the wise and knowledge to those who have understanding. He reveals deep and secret things; He knows what is in the darkness and the light dwell with Him, for His dominion and His kingdom from

generation to generation. All the inhabitant of the earth are reputed as nothing. He does according to His will in the army of heaven. And among the inhabitants of the earth, No one can restore His hand and say to him what have you done – *Dan. 2:20 – 22; Dan. 4:34-35.*

4.   I love life I do not fear death. I know of no one who can possibly want to live more than I do. My home life and marriage is happy, my future is bright and getting brighter. My health is good.

5.   I am led by the Holy Spirit and not the Law of Moses.

6.   As Jesus is so I am in this world. Jesus was never sick, so I am not sick and diseased. Jesus was not poor, so I can't be poor, I am Wealthy.

7.   I operate in the Blood covenant; I am immune to all your wickedness.

8.   I submit myself therefore to God, I resist the devil and he flees from me, praise God I am set free – *James. 4:7*

9.   And I am complete in Him, who is the head of all principalities and powers – *Col. 2:10*

10.   And the peace of God which passeth all understanding, shall keep your heart and minds through Christ Jesus our Lord – *Phil. 4:7.*

CHAPTER SEVEN

DIVINE HEALTH AND HEALING

1. My body is the home (temple) of the Holy Spirit. God lives within me, He bought it with a great price. Therefore I am a vessel of glory to God. I live above sin, diseases and all works of the enemy – *1ˢᵗ Cor. 6:19-20.*

2. The same power of God that raised Christ from the dead is at work in my physical body. It destroys all sickness and diseases, fears, germs. No infirmity, bacteria/viruses or signs and symptoms of disease is permitted in my body. The eternal life of God revitalizes and rejuvenates my mortal body. I am immune to disease and pain. I am the healed of the Lord – *1ˢᵗ Cor. 6:14*

3. My body is parts and members of Christ. Its disease and death free I enjoy and live in divine health.

4.   Bless the Lord Oh my soul, who heals all my diseases.

5.   My healing shall spring forth speedily – *Isa. 58:8*

6.   I am more than a conqueror over sickness, death, poverty, sin etc through Christ who strengthens me.

7.   By His stripes I am healed, therefore I possess healing and divine health.

8.   He Himself took my infirmities (name it) and bore my sicknesses, therefore I am free from sickness and diseases, because they were all borne by Jesus Christ for me – *Matt. 8:17*

9.   He who raised Christ from the dead will also give life to my (your) mortal body through this spirit who dwells in you (me). Therefore, I boldly say God is giving life to my mortal body now by the same spirit that

raised Jesus from the dead, because His spirit dwells in me, thus I am free from weaknesses and sicknesses.

10. My God is bigger than sickness and diseases, poverty and failure.

11. I will never be sick again; I have victory over sickness and disease.

12. I bind and cast out any spirit of infirmity and disease (name it) that is released over my family and cast it out of my life.

13. You entity, man of (call the disease) I rebuke you, I bind your works and I cast you out now, my body is not your home in Jesus name.

14. Today and always I am full of vitality and strength, the older I get, the younger I look and feel.

15. I receive wisdom to recognize faulty and disharmonious patterns of behavior,

feeding, reactions etc that I affect my health and re-adjust for overall well being.

16. My mind is immune to all negative programming that ignore my mind, feeling and response with disease and infirmity thoughts, I reject such media influences.

17. I call you ....(sickness/diseases by name) and cast you out of my body, you shall no longer operate in my body.

18. I am free from all forms of stress; I am immune to all stress influences. I live a stress free life.

19. I reject disease and I accept and receive health.

20. I reject death and every thought of it; I accept and receive long life. I will not die young but live to a long and healthy old age of...........

21. The peace of God in my life surmounts fear, doubt, worry and all weapons of the enemy.

22. I have the life of God in my mortal body.

23. Holy Spirit cleanses my body of all disease and pain.

24. Jesus Himself bore my sins on His own body on the tree, that I (we) having deed to sin might live for righteousness, by whose wounds I am healed – *1ˢᵗ Peter 2:24*

25. I have and assured lifespan of …………………years .I cover ever organ of my body in the blood of Jesus (name them),non will fail or degenerate. The older I get the more healthier and livelier I become.

26. I have a healthy life mindset/consciousness, I will live a long healthy life of ……………years

27. Good radiant health is a reality to me, as well as my rightful heritage.

28. I have a good memory, my memory is good.

29. I continually experience happiness, good health, abundance, peace and joyous expression.

30. My mind dwells only on peace, harmony, health, goodwill and not on false beliefs, fears of mankind, opinions etc.

31. I receive healing as given over 2000 years ago, by grace.

32. My feet are released, my ankles are released, my heart and lungs are relaxed, and my head is relaxed. The perfection of God is now being expressed through me. The idea of perfect health is now filling my subconscious mind. The image God has of me is a perfect image and my subconscious

mind recreates my body in perfect accordance with the perfect image held in the mind of God.

33. Christ has redeemed me from the curse of the law. Therefore I forbid any sickness or disease germ to come upon my body. Every disease germ and virus dies instantly in the name of Jesus. Every organ and every tissue of my body functions in the perfection to which God created it to function, and I forbid any malfunction in my body in the name of Jesus – *Matt. 16:19 ; Gen. 1:31*

PRAYER FOR HEALING

34. Heavenly Father I thank you that I am a believer, I am a child of God, I have been born again. I am born of God. Thou art my own father. I am thy very own child. It is written "Beloved thou art a child of God. I

am a son of God. Thank you, my father, because it is also written in thy word "Greater is He that is in you than He that is in you. The greater one is in me, it is written, I am the temple of the living God, as God has said I will dwell, I will live in them, I will walk in them. They will be my people, I will be there God, Oh Lord creator of heaven and earth, thou art my God, thou dost live in me, greater is He that is in me, than He that is in the world, he is greater than sickness, He is greater than disease, He is greater than all, He is in me, He is at work within me, for it is written in the word, who is at work within me to do and to will for His good pleasure, He is at work within me to make me whole, to heal me. It is also written that if the spirit of Him that raised up Christ dwelleth in you, He will also quicken your mortal body by His Spirit that dwelleth in you. His spirit dwelleth in me, He quickeneth my mortal body. My mortal body is made whole and full of life, my body is made full of health. He is healing me now, that life, that spirit, that power is driving out sickness from my being, health, healing, strength, life is coming into me, the cancer, the heart disease (name it) is cursed, it is dead, the symptoms, the distress of all kinds is dead. The axe is laid to the roof of this tree, every symptom, every disease, every sickness is gone, I am healed.

CHAPTER EIGHT

WELLNESS

Obesity

1. I don't desire to eat so much,lest I become over weight, I present my body to God, my body is the temple of the Holy Spirit which dwelleth in me. I am not my own, I am bought with a price, therefore I refuse to over eat, I mortify the desire of my body and command it to come in line with the Word of God.

Decree for Healing, Forgiveness, etc.

2. For sickness He has given me health.

3. I will not let the Word of God depart before my eyes for it is life to me. I have found it and it is health and healing to all my flesh – *Prov. 4:21 – 22.*

4.   I am free from unforgiveness and strife, I forgive others as Christ has forgiven me, for the love of God is shed abroad in my heart by the Holy Ghost – *Matt. 6:12; Rom. 5:5*

5.   Jesus bore my sins in His body on the tree, therefore I am dead to sin and alive unto God, and by His stripes I am healed and made whole – *1 Peter 2:24.*

6.   Jesus bore my sickness and carried my pain. Therefore I give no place to sickness or pain, for He sent His word and healed me – *Ps. 107:20*

7.   Father God because of your word I am an overcomer. I overcome the world, the flesh and the devil, by the Blood of the Lamb and the word of my testimony – *John 4:4*

8.   Lord God you have given me abundant life. I receive that life through your word and it

flows to every organ of my body bringing healing and health - *John 10:10*

9. Heavenly Father I attend to your word I incline my ears to your sayings. I will not let it depart from my eyes. I keep them in the midst of my heart, for they are life and healing to all my flesh – *Prov. 4:20-22*

10. Holy Spirit of God flushes out all ailments and infirmities from my body. I ask angelic doctors to minister to my body day and night. Replace all ailing parts from the health stores of heaven.

EYES / EARS

11. As God was with Moses, so is He with me, my eyes are not dim, neither are my nature forces abated. Blessed are my eyes for they see and my ears for the hear.

12. No evil will befall me neither shall any plague come near my dwelling, for you (God) have given your angels charge of me. They keep me in all my ways. In my pathway is life, healing and health – *Ps. 91:10, 11.*

13. Father, your word has become a part of me it is flowing in my blood stream, it flows to every cell of my body, your word has become flesh, for you sent your word and healed me, therefore I am healed of -------- (mention the ailment) – *James 1:21*

14. Your word O! God is manifested in my body causing ....disease to disappear............ disease in a thing of the past I make a demand on my body that...........function properly in Jesus name (attach the disease in the spaces) – *Mark 11:23*

15. Lord, you have blessed my food and water and have taken away sickness from me; therefore I will fulfill the number of my days in health – *Ex. 23:25, 26.*

16. I believe and receive the finished works of Jesus, Lord Jesus I thank you and receive my healing and perfect health, I live in His wholesomeness whatever cannot be found in Him cannot be found in me.

CHAPTER NINE

AT NIGHT

1. Every cell, nerve, tissue, muscle and organ of my body are now being made whole, pure and perfect. My whole body is being restored to heath and harmony now.

2. It is foolish to believe in sickness and something to hurt or harm me. I believe in perfect health, prosperity, peace, wealth and divine guidance is mine and operates in my life.

3. The image God has of me is a perfect image and my subconscious mind imbibes and believes this therefore I am being recreated in perfect accordance with the perfect image held in the mind of God.

4. It is abnormal to be sick, it is normal to be healthy; health is the truth of my being.

5.   I sought the Lord and He heard me and delivered me from all my fears – *Ps. 34:4*

6.   My body and all of its organs were created by the infinite intelligence (God) that dwells in me. He knows how to heal me, His wisdom fashioned all my organs, tissues, muscles and bones. This infinite presence within me is now transforming every atom of my being making me whole and perfect now. I give thanks for the healing I know is taking place now. Wonderful are the works of the creative intelligence within me – *Ps 139:14*

FEAR

7.   I am master over any fear. The death of fear is certain. Fear is a negative thought. I supplant it wilt a constructive thought.

Confidence is greater than fear. Nothing is more powerful than faith in God and the good.

8.   My life is self renewing, eternal, indestructible and spiritual.

9.   I am a child of infinite life, which knows no end, and I am a child of eternity, I am wonderful. I am on earth to express beauty and glory. I am happy, radiant, serene and powerful.

10.   I will not die, but live to declare the works of God – *Ps. 118:17*

11.   Father, I resist the enemy in every form that He comes against me. I require my body to be strong and healthy, and I enforce it with your word. I reject the curse and enforce life in this body – *James 4:7*

12.   Body, I speak the word of faith to you, I demand that every internal organ perform a

perfect work, for you are the temple of the Holy Ghost, therefore I charge you in the name of Jesus Christ and by the authority of His Holy word to healed and made whole in Jesus name – *Pro. 12:18*

13.   I make a demand on my ………… (Name area/organ) to function perfectly, there will be no pain or problem in my…………… ………i Refuse to allow anything that will hurt or destroy their normal function *Prov. 17:22*

14.   Father, I make a demand on my bones to produce perfect marrow. I make a demand on the marrow to produce pure blood that will ward off sicknesses and diseases. My bones refuse any offence of the curse - *Pro. 16:24.*

15.   Jesus is the Lord of my life. Sickness and disease have no power over me. I am

forgiven and free from sin and guilty, I am dead to sin and alive unto righteousness – *Col. 1:21, 22*

16. Jesus took my infirmities and bore my sicknesses; therefore I refuse to allow sickness to dominate my body. The life of God flows within me bringing healing to every fiber of my being – Matt. 8:17; John 6:63

17. I am redeemed from the curse **(Gal. 3:13)** is flowing in my blood stream. It flows to every cell of my body restoring life and health – **Mark 11:23; Luke 17:6**

18. The life of **1 Peter 2:24** is realty in my flesh, restoring every cell of my body.

CHAPTER TEN
HEALING FOR CHRONIC AILMENT/BODY ORGANS

A. Diabetes

1. My body is the temple of the Holy Ghost. I make a demand on my body to release the right chemicals. My body is in perfect chemical balance. My pancreas secretes the proper amount of insulin for life and health
   – 1 Cor. 6:19

2. I present my body to God for it is the temple of the living God. God dwells in me and His life permeates my spirit, soul and body so that I am filled with fullness of God daily – **Rom. 12:1, 2; John 14:20**

3. Heavenly Father, through your word you have imparted your life to me, that life restores my body with every breath and every word I speak

John 6:63; Mark 11:23.

4. That which God has not planted is dissolved and rooted out of my body in Jesus name – 1st Peter 2:24 is engrafted into every fibre of my being and I am alive with the life of God – **Mark 11:23; John 6:63.**

B. Growths/Tumors/Cancer

5. Growths and tumors have no right to my body. They are a thing of the past for I am delivered from the authority of darkness – **Cor. 1:13, 14**

6. I will not die but live and declare the works of God – **Ps. 118:17**

7. I command every growth and cancer to shrink, dry up and stop spreading in my body/organ in Jesus name, the curse is lifted. You invasion of cancer, my body is not habitable for you. Spirit of cancer out now. Every cancer cell is starved of its life source and nutrients and incapable of surviving in me. I shall not die but live

C. Immune System

8. My immune system grows stronger day by day; I speak life to my immune system. I forbid confusion in my immune system. The same spirit that raised Christ from the dead dwells in me and quickens my immune system with the life and wisdom of God which guards the life and health of my

body.

D. Bones, Marrow

9. I speak to the bone and joints of my body I call you normal in Jesus name. My bones and joints will not respond to any disease for the Spirit of **1st Peter 2:24** permeate every bone and joint of my body with life and health.

10. In Jesus name I forbid my body to be deceived in any manner, body you will not be deceived by any virus or disease germ neither will you work against life or health in anyway. Every cell of my body supports life and health **(Matt. 12:23, 35)**

11. The same spirit that raised Jesus from the

dead dwells in me, permeating His life through my veins, sending healing throughout my body. **Roms. 8:11**

12. The law of the Spirit of life in Christ Jesus has made me free from the law of sin and death, therefore I will not allow sin, sickness or death, it over me **(Roms. 8:2; Roms. 6:13, 14)**

E. Heart/Arteries/Cells

13. In Jesus name my arteries will not shrink or become clogged arteries! You are clean, elastic and function as God created you to function – **Luke 17:6; Mark 11:23; Isa. 55:11**

14. I am redeemed from the curse of the law and

my heart beats with the rhythm of life. The spirit and life of God's word flows in me cleansing my blood of every disease and impurity – **Prov. 4:20 -23.**

15. Every cell that does not promote life and health in my body is cut off from its life source. My immune system will not allow tumors and growths to live in my body in Jesus name – **Luke 17:6**

16. I have a strong heart, every heartbeat floods my body with life and cleanses me of disease and pain – **Ex. 23:25; Mark 11:23**

17. My heartbeat is normal. My heartbeats with the rhythm of life carrying life and health

abundantly **(John 17:23; Eph. 2:22).**

F. Arthritis/Tumors

18. Arthritis you must go! Sickness must flee. Tumors can't exist in me for the spirit of God is upon me and the word of God is within me sickness, fear and oppression have no power over me for God's word is my confession. **(Mark 11:23).**

19. Heavenly father, as I give voice to your word, the law of the spirit in Christ Jesus makes me free from the law of sin and death. And your life is energizing every cell of my body – **Rom. 8:12**

G. Intestinal System

20. My intestinal/digestive system is working perfectly .My mind is free from all forms of anxiety therefore all forms of ulcers are gone

for good.I am never constipated. My digestive system works perfectly. My system is immune to diarrhea etc.

CHAPTER ELEVEN

RELATIONSHIP, CAREER, BUSINESS, MINISTRY, SUCCESS, PROSPERITY, FINANCES

1. I receive the help of the Holy Spirit for Ministry, for business and relationships.

2. I can do all things through Christ who strengthens me – **Phil. 4:3**

3. Lord God you have made me to have dominion over the works of your and. You have put all things under my feet. Ps 8:6

4. God shall supply all my needs according to riches in Christ Jesus, therefore I possess God's supply for my every need – **Phil. 4:19**

5. I am linked with God; I cannot fail in life or in any endeavour, because God cannot fail.

6. You shall serve the Lord your God and He will bless your bread and water, and he will take sickness away from the midst of you. Therefore sickness is taken away from me and my bread and water are blessed because I am serving the Lord my God.

7. Because I have received Jesus Christ as my Savior and Lord, I have that abundant life in me now. I know God is prospering my life. I have a right to prosperity and health, and I am prospering in my soul.

8. Father God, let there be a manifestation of signs and wonders through my life by your power in all areas of my life such as my career, business and ministry.

9. Father God, let my life manifest infallible and irrevocable proofs that are discernable to all as blessings in Jesus name – **Acts. 1:3**

10. Father God, let my business, my career or my ministry etc, manifest infallible proofs of your blessings in Jesus name – **Acts. 1:8**

11. I praise the Father, God who has blessed me with every blessing in heaven because I belong to Christ – **Eph. 1:3**

12. I am asset to the Kingdom of God, and an asset to my generation.

13. I receive the Anointing of God which removes strains, eradicates stresses and refreshes me. This anointing ensures that I

ascend my God ordained throne, where everything answers to me at all times.

14. I receive spiritual insight above all challenges and circumstances of life.

15. I reject poverty and lack; I receive and accept prosperity and wealth in my life. I grow in wealth.

16. I am a vessel of mercy prepared for glory before the foundation of the world; I take hold of my prosperous inheritance in God.

17. I am positioned as a sign and wonder to the world.

18. I belong to Christ therefore I carry a life giving fragrance.

19. I am a vessel of joy I bring happiness to all who come in contact with me.

20. The Lord is prospering and watering my life, for by His grace. I am a generous and cheerful giver – **Prov. 11:23**

21. God is my God and He has prepared for me a beautiful city - Heb. 11:16

22. I am rich, I am wealthy.

23. I expand my circle of profitable friendships for helpful relationships.

24.   I am rich in material goods, money, houses. I am rich in mental and spiritual blessings. I am rich in personal power and leadership, I am rich in friendships.

25.   I have accepted the idea that I am a success.

26.   I take full advantage of the great source of intelligence and power contained within my mind.

27.   I have a success consciousness. I am a success in every area of life, I am a success.

28. I have a magnetic and charming personality, quality people are automatically drawn to me.

29. I see myself as a success not a failure success surrounds me and comes to me automatically and naturally.

30. I can be a success.

    ↓

    I will be a success

    ↓

    I am a success

    ↓

    I have a success mindset

31. I am twice as good as I think I am.

32. I am able to drive a better car, build a dream home, etc.

33. I have within me, a mental make-up that has all that is necessarily to enable me to form ideas which will have a definite value to humanity and which at the same time will reap handsome rewards for me.

34. My mind is alert and active, continually bringing into my consciousness a flow of constructive ideas of value to humanity.

35. I have a wealthy person's consciousness and mindset. I have a multi millionaire's mindset and attitude.

36. I see myself in a bigger and better house that is elegantly furnished I have and drive the finest automobiles. My children are in the finest schools and colleges. I travel the world. (Create & speak your desire).

37. I will be divinely guided in thought and action towards the solution of my problem. (Name it) it will be easy and fun to get ………….. Amount of money every month.

38. I direct my creative mind/faculties to assist me in the solving of problems; to help me make the right decisions to create ways and means of great achievement.

39.	Six --------months from today (name it) I will be a multimillionaire etc. I will earn ……………monthly.

40.	I command you my prosperity Angels to bring my money in millions of naira etc. I command my prosperity angels to bring me prosperous connections.

41.	I call forth my (what number)destiny helpers for business and career

42.	There is never any shortage of the blessings God is willing and anxious to bestow upon me. I receive them gladly.

43.	My mind is free from any mental block against abundance, wealth and prosperity.

44. Money cometh to me now from the East, West, North and South now in Jesus name. The city of -------- is delivered to me , I shall eat the good of the land

45. I earn ....Naira/Dollar etc. Every single month of ....year.

46. I have more than enough in my finances, I command my Angels of abundance to work.

47. The hundred fold return is working for me now. I discover my place of increase and I walk in abundance today.

48. I receive divine inspiration for a business etc and set plans to succeed, Holy Spirit show me.

49. I have a circle of admiring friends, I am a power in my community, I represent authority. Have a personality that conveys leadership and influence.

50. There is a gold mine within me from which I can extract everything I need to live gloriously, joyously and abundantly. Whatever I want I can draw forth.

51. I am a woman/man who is full of faith and confidence, I am born to win and succeed. I am winning and succeeding day by day.

52. Through God's grace I bring into my life more power, more wealth, more health, and more happiness by God's provision for me.

53. God is imparting to me now wonderful kinds of knowledge and wisdom for success in life. I am receptive to new ideas etc.

54. I come into actual possession of the power and wisdom necessary to move forward in abundance, security, joy and dominion.

55. I am living in a fathomless sea of infinite riches.

56. I believe and receive the finished works of Jesus. Lord Jesus I thank you and receive --- ----- my healing and perfect health, my

wealth and prosperity, my spiritual maturity, I live in God's righteousness.

57. I am blessed when I go out; I am blessed when I come in. I am blessed in the field; I am blessed in the city.

58. Infinite intelligence by God leads and guides me in all my ways. Perfect health is mine and the law of harmony operates in my mind and body, beauty love, peace and abundance are mine. The principle of right action and divine order govern my life totally. I know my major premise is based on the eternal truths of life and I know, feel and believe that my subconscious mind responds according to the nature of my conscious mind thinking.

59.   Divine power and His wisdom is at work in my subconscious mind guiding, directing and prospering me spiritually, mentally and materially.

60.   The divine intelligence of God who gave me the desire (Name it) leads, guides and reveals to me the perfect plan for the unfolding of my desire. I know the deeper wisdom of my subconscious in now responding, and what I feel and claim within is expressed in the without. There is balance, equilibrium and equanimity.

61.   God is the source of my supply. The blessing of Abraham is my source. I have no limit to my income.

62. The Lord is my shepherd I shall not lack.

63. I believe that the power of God that created me has also given me the desire for wealth, health and success, is now fulfilling it through me. All conflicts are dissolved.

64. I know the plans God has for me. As declared by the Lord plans to prosper me and not harm me. Plans to give me hope and a future.

65. My life is so easy, life is good, and all good things come to me.

66. I deserve all good things life has to offer, all good things are my birth right.

67.   This is a magnificent universe created by a magnificent God; He is bringing all good things to me. God is conspiring for me in all things; He is supporting me in everything I do. All my needs are met consistently.

68.   Christ has redeemed me from poverty.

69.   I delight myself in the Lord and He gives me the desire of my heart –Ps. 37:4

70.   I have given and it is given unto me good measure, pressed down, shaken together, running over, men give unto my bosom – Luke 6:38

71.   With what measure I mete (give), it is measured unto me. I sow bountifully;

therefore I reap bountifully. I give cheerfully and my God has made all grace abound towards me, and I have all sufficiency of all things, I do abound to all good works – **2 Cor. 9:6-8**

72.   There is no lack for my Good supplieth all of my needs according to His riches in glory by Jesus Christ – **Phil. 4:19**

73.   The Lord is my shepherd and I do not want because Jesus was made poor that through his poverty I might have abundance. For He came that I might have life and have it more abundantly – **Ps. 23:1; John 10:10**

74.   The Lord has pleasure in the prosperity of His servant, Abrahams blessing are mine – **Gal. 3:14.**

75.   The spirit of truth abideth in me and teaches me all things, and guides me into all truths therefore I confess I have perfect knowledge of every circumstance that I come up against, for I have the wisdom of God - **(John 16:13).**

76.   In my career in my business, I trust in the Lord with all my heart and I lean not unto my own understanding. In all my ways I acknowledge Him and He directs all my path – **Pro. 3:5-6**

77. I let the Word of Christ dwell in me richly in all wisdom – Col. 3:16.

A. To Eliminate Debt

78. In Jesus name and on the authority of His holy word, I call these debts (name it) paid in full, debt I speak to you in Jesus name be paid and be gone. Dematerialize and cease to exist. I now declare that all my debts, mortgages and notes are now paid in full, cancelled or dissolved.

B. To Collect Money Owed

79. (Make a list of your debtors and lay hands on them). Jesus said whatever I loose on earth is loosed in heaven; therefore I loose

the finances that are owed to me. I call this money in so that these accounts are paid in Jesus name **(Matt. 18:18)**

C. Timely Payment of Bills

80. (Put your bills in a stack lay your hands upon them and declare out loud) God supplies all my needs according to His riches in glory by Christ Jesus. God is the source of my supply, and I have more than enough to pay my bills in time, bills be paid in full – *Phil. 4:19*

D. To Sell Property/Community

(Make Sure Your Price Is Fair – Prov. 20:23)

81. Talk to it and say listen to me. I am talking to you. Jesus said you would obey me. You

are going to be a blessing to someone and I call you sold in Jesus name.

E. To Buy Property

82. I call those things that are not as though they were. I now call the property that fits my needs and desire and will be a blessing to me. I call you to me now in Jesus name. I declare that Gods highest and best is done in this matter and the Angels are now working on my behalf – *Rom. 4:17*

F. To Meet and Surpass Set Targets

83. I can do all things through Christ who strengthens me from within, therefore this week, this month I surpass my sales and business targets. God will cause me to come in contact with Kings and Princes who will patronize and grant me my request. I prosper by favor and not struggle.

84. The blessing of the Lord makes me truly rich and adds no sorrow with it – *Prov. 10:22*

85. Wherever my feet enters I shall possess- *Joshua 1:3*

86. The heart of kings and princes belong to God ,therefore the will favor me, every word of request is granted

87. I receive the sum of ---- and this month of ------ I send out my angels ahead of me

G. To Remove Hindrance

88. God your Word says that whatever I bind on earth is bound in heaven and whatever I loose on earth is loosed in heaven, therefore on the authority of your Word, I bind every force that has set itself against my financial prosperity. I hereby declare all curses against me null, void and harmless! I am redeemed from the curse of poverty. I am

free from oppression! I now loose the abundance of God and all that rightfully belongs to me now comes to me under grace in a perfect way.

89. To increase your salary (work with diligence, tithe in advance for your raise or promotion), hold your paycheck in your hand and say – Heavenly Father, I call for a raise as I honor you with the 1st fruit of my increase. I give thanks for this job and bless my employer. I now declare that this check multiplies and is increased. I am now richly rewarded for my work both creatively and financially. By the month of----- or year of, I will earn --------

H. To Increase Your Investment and Bank Accounts

90. I call for abundance as I honor the Lord with my capital and sufficiency my storage

places (investments and bank accounts) are filled with plenty and my presses burst forth with now wine. I am abundantly supplied – *Pro. 3:9, 10.*

I. For Employment

91. I now dissolve and put aside all negative, limiting beliefs about where I will work and what kind of work is available to me. I open myself to all of God's possibilities. I call for a perfect, satisfying, well-paying job to manifest in my life. I am always in the right place at the right time for the Spirit of God directs my steps – *Prov. 16:9; Rom. 5:17*

92. Father I thank you I will start a job by the 1st week of the month of --------- for the whole earth and its fullness belong to you (all companies and organizations) The hearts of Kings and princes is in your hand (MDs,

CEOs, etc).I call up my divine contact, settings and opportunities concerning my new job. It is delivered to me latest --------- (put down date or month of your expectation).

CHAPTER TWELVE

PROGRAMMING YOUR SPIRIT FOR SUCCESS

1. I am filled with the knowledge of God's will in all wisdom and spiritual understanding. His will is my prosperity – *Col. 1:19*

2. God delights in my prosperity, He gives me power to get wealth, that He may establish His covenant upon the earth – *Deut. 8:18, 11, 12*

3. I immediately respond in faith to the guidance of the Holy Spirit within me. I am always in the right place at the right time because my steps are ordered of the Lord.

4. God has given me all things that pertain to life and Godliness, and I am well able to

possess all that God has provided for me –
Num. 13:30; 2 Peter 1:3, 4

5.   As I give it is given unto me, good measure pressed down, shaken together and running over – *Luke 6:38.*

6.   I honor the Lord with my substance and the first fruits of my increase, my barns are filled with plenty, and my presses burst forth with new win – *Pro. 3:9, 10.*

7.   I am like a tree planted by the rivers of water. I bring forth fruit in my season, my leaf shall not wither, and whatever I do will prosper. The grace of God makes my mistakes to prosper – *Ps. 1:3*

8. I am blessed in the city, I am blessed in the field, I am blessed coming in and blessed going out. I am blessed in the basket and blessed in the store, my bank accounts, investments, health and relationships flourish. The blessings of the Lord overtakes me in all areas of my life – *Deut. 28:1-14.*

9. My God makes all grace abound towards me in every favor and earthly blessing, so that I have all sufficiency for all things and abound to every good work – *2 Cor. 9:8*

10. The Lord has pleasure in the prosperity of His servant, and Abrahams blessings are mine – *Ps. 35:27; Gal. 3:14*

11. Having received the abundance of grace and gift of righteousness, I reign as a King in life by Jesus Christ *(Roms. 5:17).*

CHAPTER THIRTEEN

MARRIAGE/FAMILY BLESSING

1. I experience perfect harmony in my marriage; I love my wife/husband and experience marital bliss and wholeness. I am irresistibly attracted physically to my wife/husband.

2. I am attractive and charming to my wife/husband. I am making her/him happy and she/him is in turn will make me happy and meet all of my desires.

3. I am divinely happy in my marriage.

4. I have a magnetic personality; I naturally do all of the things which will attract a spouse for me.

5. In the next -------- month I will come in contact with my would be wife or husband, we shall recognize each other and be connected. We will be spiritually, mentally

and physically compatible. .I will have my wedding on --------- date.

6. Father I thank you that I am a helper therefore send me to a man I will help to fulfill divine destiny. I come in contact with such man in the next ---- month and by ---- month I will be married to him. I bind any abortion of destiny forces and enemies of marriage. I am free from evil veils, offensive spiritual odors, I have attractive fragrance that attracts the man of my dreams.

FAMILY BLESSINGS

1.   Sickness is taken away from me and family because we serve the Lord – **Exo. 23:25**

2.   Great is the peace of my children because they are taught of the Lord – **Isa. 54:13**

3.   No evil shall befall my children/family, neither shall any plague come near there dwelling for God has given His angels charge of them. To keep them in all there ways in there pathway is life, success, healing and health – **Ps. 91:10, 11**

4.   All the talents and capabilities of my children will be realized in there life. Every generational curse stops and will not materialize in their life. I will not bury any of them. They will be a blessing and not a sorrow to me and their world. The will be solution providers to their world. What

consumes children at young age is defeated in their life

5. I call forth the family blessings for my family ordained before the foundation of the world. This family will be fruitful, prosperous and safe.

6. The enemies of the first child/son and last child will not prevail over them.

7. As a parent I will not bury my children nor die young. At old age my children will surround my table. I will carry my grand-children and enjoy the fruits; I will not be a widow or widower. I will not be killed; I will not be a victim. It is so to my spouse and children. Accidents and harm are far from us. We shall not be victims.

REFERENCES/SOURCES

1. Dr. Creflo Dollar

2. Charles Capps

3. Rev. Kenneth Hagin

All materials from the above persons/ministries for this book are in form of excerpts from books, seminars, ds (audio and visual),tracts, podcasts, Facebook comments and personal notes at conferences etc, All duly acknowledged without intent of abuse and alterations.

CONTACT

We have developed seminars and training programmes for individuals, businesses, church and schools in form of audio, videos/CDs, manuals, etc that are for personnel and corporate growth.

Audio version of this book is also available.

Contact us for speaking, counseling, training engagements .

Call: +2348028383477

E-mail: network4helpers@gmail.com

ABOUT THE BOOK

It looks like a promise that may not be granted, a promise untrue. However what we say really matters, how we say it, when we say it and our consistency at it.

In this book, you are guide to leverage on faith and your part towards changing your life circumstances and determining its outcome as you speak right and authoritatively to activate the supernatural and spiritual.

Reprogramme your mind for tangible positive outcome such as healing, prosperity, success, harmonious relationship, deliverance and spiritual growth etc.

ABOUT THE AUTHOR

Munachimso Nwosu obtained academic qualifications in Psychology and Education from University of Nigeria, Nsukka and the National Teachers Institute, Nigeria respectively. He is a highly experienced life and business coach, a healthy living practitioner, entrepreneur, author, poet. His passion is to help people, communities, organizations discover and maximize potential and purpose. He is currently the President and Founder of Delight Family Life Foundation/Club and Entheos Heritage Leadership and Success Center in Nigeria which plans and host all-year programs locally and internationally. The center promotes growth, harmony and success for all aspects of family life, communities, organizations etc. He is happily married to Chijindu and they have 3 Children; Zoe, David and Oganihu.

www.ingramcontent.com/pod-product-compliance
Lightning Source LLC
Chambersburg PA
CBHW032041040426

42449CB00007B/966